Because the Fable

ISBN 978-1-0980-8282-6 (paperback)
ISBN 978-1-0980-8283-3 (digital)

Christian Faith Publishing, Inc.
832 Park Avenue
Meadville, PA 16335
www.christianfaithpublishing.com

Printed in the United States of America

Because the Fable

William Milligan

On this night came Jesus

And throughout the stable

Every creature was prancing

It was because of the fable

It was foretold that a
Savior would be born
And He would be an heir
To King David's throne

From the family line
Of the blessed Abraham
He was to travel
All across the land

From the tribes of Judah
A prophet to be anointed
The Messiah would arrive
He was Divinely appointed

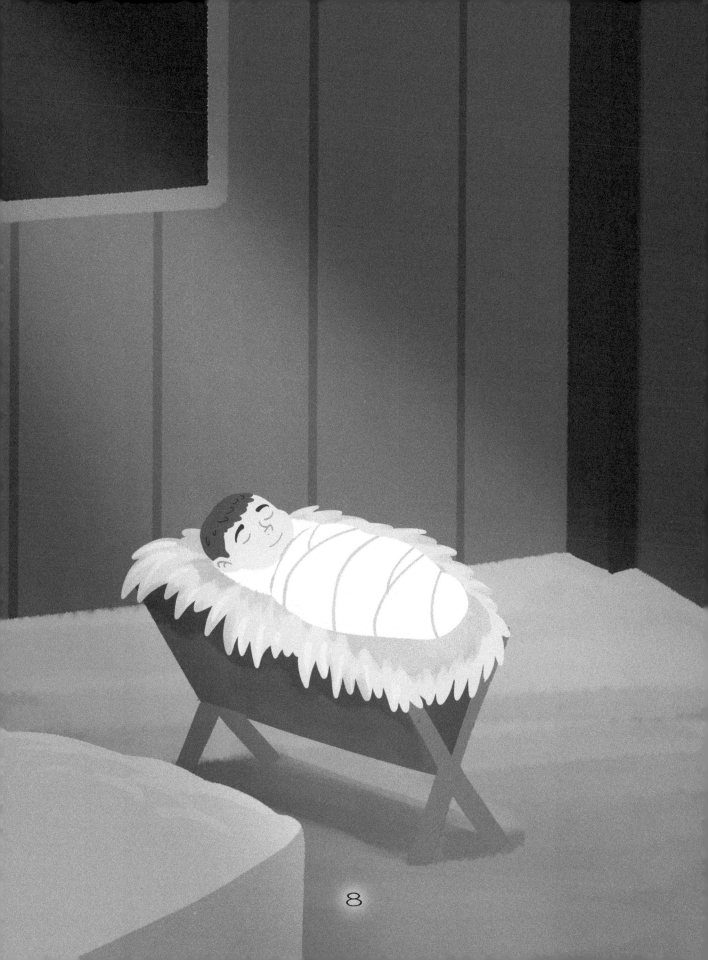

9

The son of Mary would spread his grand message
From the Father above
And of the Holy Spirit
Who descends like a dove

Jesus is God's gift

His light and His Glory

Pay homage to Him

And retell this wondrous story

13

This Noel is majestic
Exciting and yes fun
But there would be no Santa Claus
Without Jesus, God's Son

So in this Holy Season

And on this great day

Remember that Christmas is Jesus

And in His name, we pray

16

Happy Birthday Jesus
And a very Merry Christmas to you!

About the Author

William Milligan is a married, father of two who enjoys writing and playing music. His work in the IT industry has taken him to many states and thirty countries around the globe. Oftentimes he can be found playing guitar at parties and making up silly songs to get the children to smile and dance. His fourth-grade teacher wrote on his final report card that she would see his name as an author someday—and look at him now! Deft and humorous storytelling runs throughout his family, which may partly explain his penchant for the written word—so he can remember what was said!